AMAGING MIGRATIONS

ON THE MOVE WITH LEATHERBACK SEA TURTLES

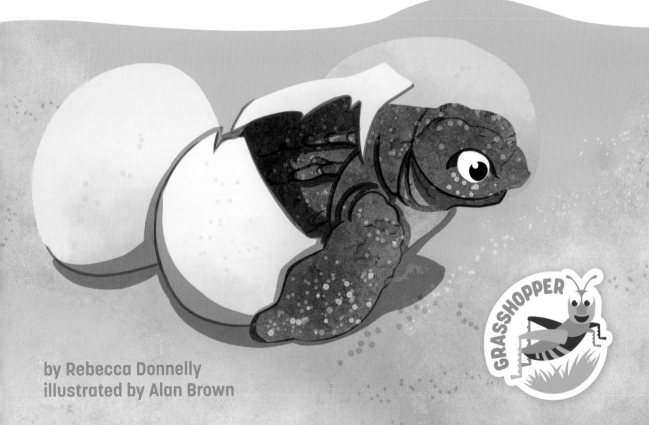

by Rebecca Donnelly
illustrated by Alan Brown

Tools for Parents & Teachers

Grasshopper Books enhance imagination and introduce the earliest readers to fiction with fun storylines and illustrations. The easy-to-read text supports early reading experiences with repetitive sentence patterns and sight words.

Before Reading

• Discuss the cover illustration. What do readers see?

• Look at the glossary together. Discuss the words.

Read the Book

• Read the book to the child, or have him or her read independently.

• "Walk" through the book and look at the illustrations. Who is the main character? What is happening in the story?

After Reading

• Prompt the child to think more. Ask: Lucia accidentally eats a plastic bag in the ocean, thinking it's a jellyfish. Why do you think she mistook the plastic bag for food?

Grasshopper Books are published by Jump!
5357 Penn Avenue South
Minneapolis, MN 55419
www.jumplibrary.com

Library of Congress Cataloging-in-Publication Data

Names: Donnelly, Rebecca, author.
Brown, Alan, illustrator.
Title: On the move with leatherback sea turtles Rebecca Donnelly; illustrated by Alan Brown.
Description: Minneapolis, MN: Jump!, Inc., [2023]
Series: Amazing migrations | Includes index.
Audience: Ages 7-10
Identifiers: LCCN 2021060754 (print)
LCCN 2021060755 (ebook)
ISBN 9781636908885 (hardcover)
ISBN 9781636908892 (paperback)
ISBN 9781636908908 (ebook)
Subjects: LCSH: Leatherback turtle–Migration–Juvenile literature.
Migratory animals–Juvenile literature.
Classification: LCC QL666.C546 D66 2023 (print)
LCC QL666.C546 (ebook)
DDC 597.92/89–dc23/eng/20220110
LC record available at https://lccn.loc.gov/2021060754
LC ebook record available at https://lccn.loc.gov/2021060755

Editor: Eliza Leahy
Direction and Layout: Anna Peterson
Illustrator: Alan Brown

Printed in the United States of America at Corporate Graphics in North Mankato, Minnesota.

Table of Contents

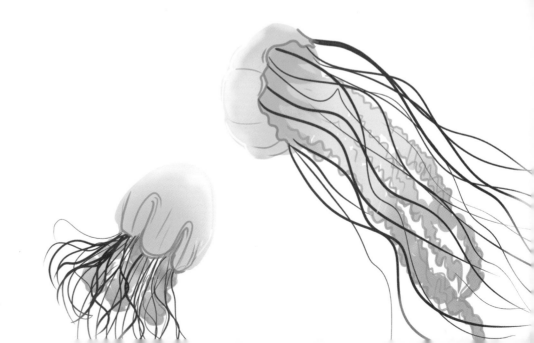

An Ocean Journey

Hi there! I'm Lucia. I'm a leatherback sea turtle hatchling. I just hatched from my egg on this beach in Panama.

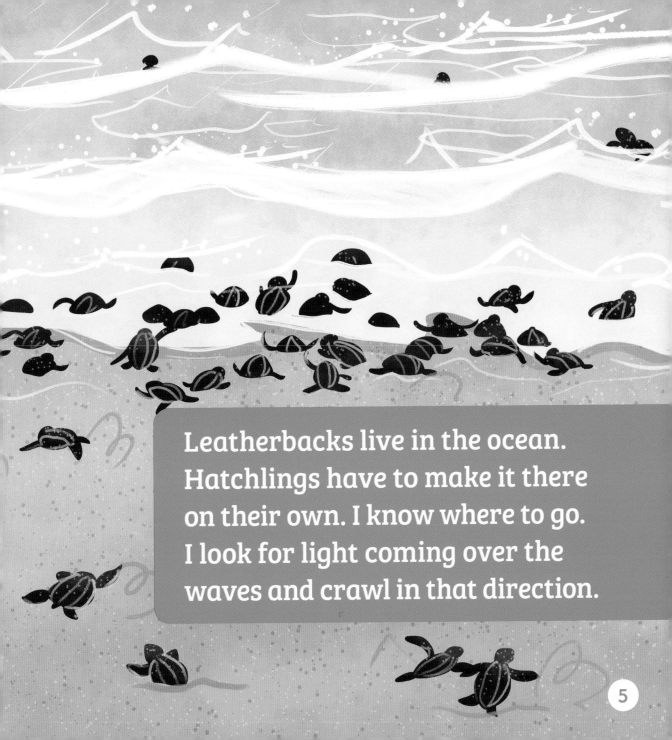

Leatherbacks live in the ocean. Hatchlings have to make it there on their own. I know where to go. I look for light coming over the waves and crawl in that direction.

Into the Atlantic Ocean I go! I find food for myself, like seaweed and small jellyfish. I try to avoid predators.

You won't see me again until I'm old enough to migrate back here to mate and nest. That will be in about 10 years!

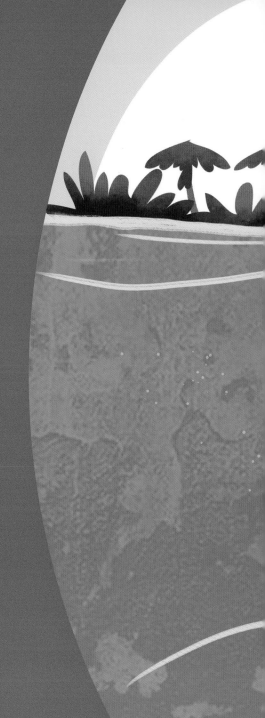

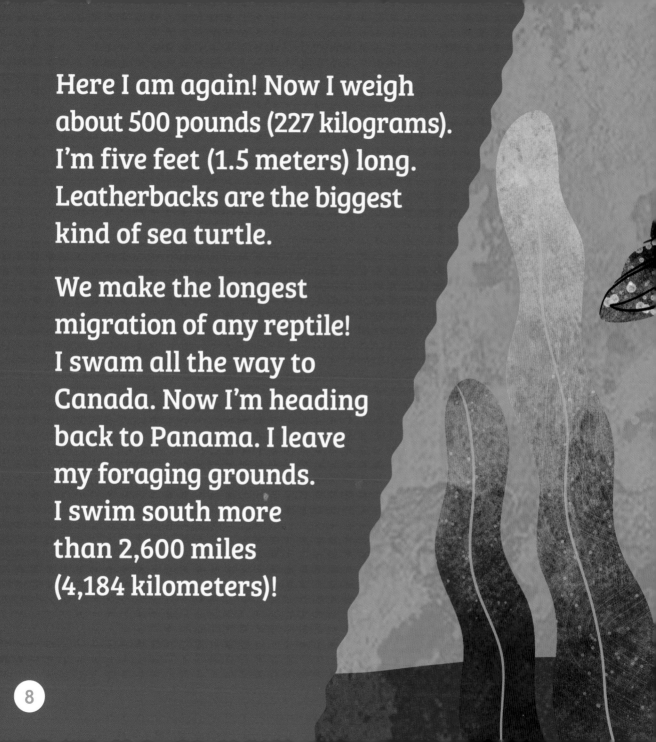

Here I am again! Now I weigh about 500 pounds (227 kilograms). I'm five feet (1.5 meters) long. Leatherbacks are the biggest kind of sea turtle.

We make the longest migration of any reptile! I swam all the way to Canada. Now I'm heading back to Panama. I leave my foraging grounds. I swim south more than 2,600 miles (4,184 kilometers)!

I start my migration in December. Other female leatherbacks migrate, too, but we travel alone.

I eat invertebrates along the way. This jellyfish tastes funny. Oh, no! It's a plastic bag. Yuck! I hate when that happens. Plastic is bad for sea creatures.

There aren't many dangers in the open ocean. But as I get close to shore, I have to watch out for fishing lines. I could get caught on the hooks.

12

I watch for fishing nets, too. Thousands of turtles get caught in them every year. I don't want to be one of them!

In March, I arrive near
Panama. Many male
leatherbacks are here.
They are big! We will
mate in the ocean, but
we won't stay together.

I am ready to lay eggs. I dig my first nest on this beach. I dig it deep in the sand so my eggs will be safe.

I lay my eggs at night. There are more than 100 of them! If the sand is warm, my hatchlings will be females. If it is cool, they will be males. In about 10 days, I'll dig another nest and lay more eggs. I'll nest five times.

Between laying eggs,
I go in the ocean. A tiger
shark waits near the
beach! Its sharp teeth
can bite through a turtle.
But I turn my carapace
toward it. Not so easy
to bite through my shell!

carapace ·····▶

It's the end of nesting season. I'll swim back to my foraging grounds. I'll stay in the open ocean for two or three years. Then I will be ready to mate again.

My hatchlings won't come with me. They will have to look out for themselves, just like I did!

Migration Map

Lucia lives and migrates in the Atlantic Ocean. Take a look!

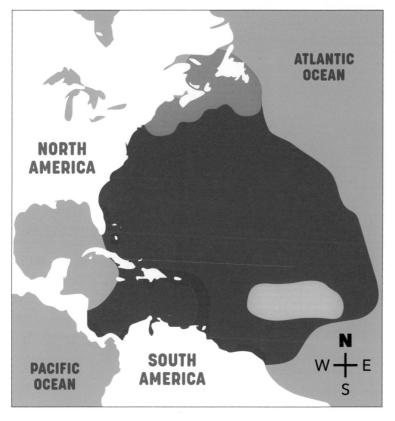

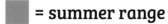 = summer range

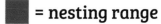 = nesting range

= migration range

= winter foraging range

Let's Review!

Why does Lucia migrate from Canada to Panama?

A. to find jellyfish to eat   **B.** to avoid sharks
C. to avoid fishing nets   **D.** to mate and lay eggs

Glossary

carapace: The shell of a turtle. A leatherback's carapace is covered with thick skin.

foraging grounds: The areas where animals look for food.

hatchling: A baby sea turtle.

invertebrates: Animals that don't have backbones.

mate: To join together to produce young.

migrate: To move from one area to another at certain times of the year.

predators: Animals that hunt other animals for food.

reptile: A cold-blooded animal that crawls across the ground or creeps on short legs.

Let's Review! Answer Key: **A.** to find jellyfish to eat **D.** to mate and lay eggs

23

Index

To Learn More

FACT SURFER

Finding more information is as easy as 1, 2, 3.

❶ Go to www.factsurfer.com

❷ Enter "**onthemovewithleatherbackseaturtles**" into the search box.

❸ Choose your book to see a list of websites.